T5-BCI-431

ATLANTIS
Selected Poems 1953-1982

Slavko Mihalić

Translated by
Charles Simic and Peter Kastmiler

ATLANTIS
Selected Poems 1953-1982

ACKNOWLEDGMENTS

Grateful acknowledgment is made to *The Literary Review*, *Modern Poetry in Translation*, and the anthologies *Contemporary Yugoslav Poetry*, University of Iowa Press, and *Contemporary East European Poetry*, by Ardis, where earlier versions of several of these poems have appeared.

Copyright © 1983 by Charles Simic & Peter Kastmiler

ISBN: 0-912678--61-5

Greenfield Review Chapbook # 61

Library of Congress Catalogue Card # 83-81610

Greenfield Center, N.Y.
The Greenfield Review Press

CONTENTS

INTRODUCTION

> *"Who in the future wishes to find out the truth about our age, or who decides to write, for whatever reason, its true history, will not find anywhere more reliable testimony than in poetry."*
>
> Antun Šoljan

> *"We want historians to confirm our belief that the present rests upon profound intentions and immutable necessities. But the true historical sense confirms our existence among countless lost events without a landmark or a point of reference."*
>
> Michel Foucault

The world is still, as Slavko Mihalić knows, false and cruel and beautiful. Born in 1928, he belongs with Zbigniew Herbert, Miroslav Holub, and great many other East European poets, to a generation that survived an epoch of unimaginable violence. There is no question that these poets have felt and thought about the evil in our century more acutely than their contemporaries in the West. Mihalić speaks of that day when, in a moment of clarity, one did finally ask "about our destiny which kept making more and more inconsiderate demands while paying less and less attention to me." He is the poet of that knowledge, the full weight of that knowledge. What makes the poems moving is that the poet's fate is of course our fate too.

Mihalić is an urban poet in the same sense that Catullus, Apollinaire, and Frank O'Hara are unthinkable without their cities. Nature with its sights and creatures is a lovely and yet, somehow, less real presence for the poet. The city he speaks of repeatedly is Zagreb, but it could be any other rapidly grown medium-sized town where even the native inhabitant feels estranged. Mihalić's poet is a pedestrian. He paces the city as if measuring it again and again. From time to time he stops at a cafe. Wine is brought to the table. The poet looks around, studies the people, thinks. There is a kind of awe in this poetry before the strangeness of the familiar. How strange, indeed, everything is! That's what lyric poetry has said since the Greeks. The poets

ix

abandoned the biographies of gods for their own. This is where their transgression lies and their solitude.

Our selection attempts to give the flavor of what is a large body of work. I count some fourteen books of poetry. An equally interesting selection could have been made from the many other fine poems. Perhaps this recent poem is the best introduction to the poet and his work. It's entitled "Second Class Citizen." It shows the kind of heroic constitution one needs to live this century.

He made peace with eternity,
and that's why his name, perhaps,
has been crossed out from the list
of those equal before the law.

At night with burning eyes
he speaks of ancestries and origins
on the other side of the cosmic ocean,
and that's why, perhaps,
there's no room for him at the feast table of the world-wise.

Always before locked doors,
bit by bit he forgets human speech.
What could he say to those
who substituted power for sense,
violence for love?

The birds and flowers of the fields
are happy, greeting him
just the way the stars do.
That's where his home is:
nowhere and everywhere.

And perhaps, truly,
one day he'll be the guide
to the dead rulers of the world.
Restrained and smiling,
he'll show them their places
in the well-earned oblivion.

Charles Simic
June 1983

COAT OF ARMS

OUR ANCIENT FAMILY SIGN

Travelling thus with a hip-flask of fierce wine,
I kissed big fat mamas in delicious daydreams.

My soul sang in a cage gone rusty.
With a cardboard sword I cut the villains down.

Who wouldn't plead to have that life all over again.
Penniless, it seemed, I had bought everything.

OAT OF ARMS

And above the door our ancient family sign:
Black gallows and a greasy rope.

1

METAMORPHOSIS

I would like to know from where
this emptiness comes, so that I
can change myself into a clear lake
where the bottom can be seen, but without fish.

But without shells, crabs, without
the underwater plants which at least
hide some kind of name, today I am
nameless. Some of me is already disappearing.

And so, speaking of emptiness, I stir
the water in the lake,
scattering sand and other tiny particles
settled on the bottom. I'm feeling nauseous.

I walk the streets with my head down,
just like another lake, first dark, afterwards
even polluted; and let's not say anything of those
repulsive creatures that crawl on the bottom
so that now I stink even to myself.

PASTORAL

My world is small,
Yet when I dive into it,
It seems bottomless.

At times I rule there,
At times it eludes me cleverly,
Then I call it with my flute.

If I happen to play the wrong song,
Strange sounds are heard,
Little demons rally around me.

They chase me over thorns, stumps,
And over some kind of sharp rock,
My bare feet bleed.

Where goat-paths come to an end,
Chasms open before me,
Cold winds whip me.

The little demons
Run leapfrog over each other,
They can go into the sky or into the earth.

Surely a bad end is in store for me,
But I hear the leading goat's bell
Right behind my back.

FOREST VISIT

With the sound of my footsteps
You grow even bigger, o forest.
In the end you'll bend over my head, gratefully.

Let the carpet be rich in color,
And there, where the eye doesn't reach,
May I stand in the festive midst
Of its fullest fragrance.

Somewhere underneath it all,
The paper and pen fell.
Then the song of birds told me:
Night's coming.

Shall I tremble because of the old stories?
(I confided into solitude.)
Nobody ever took such good care of me.

A wolf from a fairy tale surrounded me with a wreath
    of gentleness.
He panted craving to be my friend.
In the morning, leaving the forest, I regreted
Not having found his lair.

WHAT A MIGHTY DAY

You move in as if I called for you.
Your birds romp before my door as if they were born
    right here,
And the sun, the indifferent sun, throws open
    the bars and curtains on the windows.

What a mighty day! Shall I embrace it?

If I knew what its true meaning was, I'd
    welcome it lavishly,
endowing its birds with millet or some other seed
while to its sun I offer my face as a mirror.

Instead, I wait
when it will end, discouraged.

THE GLITTER OF WAVES

My dear, why should I tell you about my worries,
So tied to the invisible changes in the sky,
And to that sea which wants to be freed of its cage,
Forests too drooping over the empty depths.

Why should I kiss you when kisses leave no traces.
Like a stone you're simple and unconquerable,
Even more remote when gripped by a lover's hand.
Your body turns gold as it offers itself naked to the sun,

The sun which is in every grain of your golden skin,
The way weariness is in all of my pores.
I don't even know whether in the end I took you,

Or did we remain silent all afternoon on the beach,
You disappointed, and I enchanted by the glitter of waves,
So in love with every curve of your body, invincible.

THE BREAD ON THE TABLE

Everything you wish to say to me, tell me
in front of this dark bread on the table.
Around it walls and stars. And all the rings
which tighten around my heart.

Before this bread, more lasting than all flags,
tell me, if you dare, your verdict.
The bread will know. I will make all fears
laughably small.

Before the bread on the table
which continuously renews itself in hope,
you may exchange my life for death.
With such bread I'd cheerfully eat death.

APPROACHING STORM

Look at those clouds Vera, why are you so silent?
For god's sake, I'm not an animal. Here comes the rain.
How quickly it has turned cold.
It's a long way back to town.

You know I'll never forget what you've given me Vera.
Yes, we are one now, so what else can we talk about?
Yellow clouds usually bring hail.
Everything is already still, the crickets and the
    wheatfields.

If you want we can even stay.
I'm afraid for you, for me it doesn't matter.
Lightning is dangerous in open fields.
We are now the highest point (and so damn alone).

Tonight farmers will be cursing the spilled grains
    and the hard rain.
I couldn't stand to be so dependent on changes.
Don't cry Vera, those are only nerves
Sensing the storm.

I tell you, life is in every respect much simpler.
Here come the first drops, soon the storm will begin,
Button up your dress Vera, look at yourself, even the
    flowers are closing.
I couldn't forgive myself if anything happened to you.

Of course this place will remain sacred in my memory.
Please walk faster Vera and stop looking back.

THE FLIGHT OF THE LOVERS

I'm telling you, we must leave immediately.
Where? That we'll decide later.
The important thing is to leave soon.
I feel my innards beginning to rot.

Our eyes have withered and hang like burnt leaves.
The heart-clock is slow—one can barely hear it.
Why should I be sorry to leave my grave?
What can I do if someone feels comfortable in it.

Come, don't make it difficult, love.
To hell with coffins—they must already be pestilent.
We won't take the road—there could be ambushes.
We'll go by air—between stars.

WITH CHAINS ON YOUR HANDS

I watch you with chains on your hands,
(This fairy tale I'll write in blood so that
    it may yet spare me,)
You put them on yourself,
And then you couldn't take them off.

For you, just for you, I say these words:
(Let them be unintelligible to others—they could
    do evil),
Don't despair because of chains,
But with them, immensely heavy as you are, go
    on your journey.

In that lies the solution to many a human error:
To act and then to say I didn't act.
To love and later to say I didn't love.
And then, of course, to shut up entirely.

A FEAST FULL OF EXPECTATIONS

I drank this wine already, sat here
Neither younger nor older, (does the spirit count?)
Raised my glass, thus, a little above my head,
Waiting for my miracle—whatever it wishes.

Precious liquid, as long as it is not used,
Drips down tricked, like rain from the roof.

Tomorrow the sun will raise it again
As high as this glass, this feast full of expectations.

Behind our backs there's someone big who mocks
    at everything,
Innocent, I guess, like a housewife plucking a rooster.

Yes, just this chair, this dreamy music.
At times one could see in the corner of the eye
All seas and lands throwing themselves toward the horizon.

How wide is the palm of the hand?
Wide enough for us to search for each other hopelessly.

THE EXILE'S RETURN

He's now the ruler of the country which once exiled him,
He's not a king or the king's minister, he just does
　　what he wants,
watching from the window the crowds of the deluded
　　roam the streets,
himself wise and handsome since he's free of purpose.

Yes, now he's like a child and also like a tomb.
At times, it seems to him, that beside two hands
　　he has wings.
But he won't fly. He knows it's enough to feel that, like the sea
which feels almighty and still doesn't
　　go about rearranging the continents.

The greatest adventure is a flower in a glass of water.
With extraordinary energy he has concentrated all his
　　faith into it.
Now, deeply just, he leans over, waiting to wither,
serenely, the way ashes fall from a cigarette.

ON THE TERRACE

Step out on the terrace and behave as you always do
this is the way one brings out a chair
this is the way one lights a candle
don't forget to pay the tax
this is the way an apple is peeled
this is the way one shrugs the shoulders
everybody steps on the terrace when they have to
the rest can control themselves and wait
forcing them might upset the order of the program
and we insist that nothing be left out
this is the way a bottle of vintage wine is opened
this is the way one waves to those leaving
they were never here and still they're leaving us
vengefully they stride toward the thinned-out woods
this is the way one drinks a glass of wine even if it is
    medicinal
it's not for us to ponder the purpose of the act
one needs to let go and that's all that matters
whatever else you imagine you are alone
on the terrace—and everything else is illusion
this is the way ghosts are summoned
this is the way one becomes a specter

A FEW OF US

for Antun Šoljan

1
Beside us surge the raging rapids of the dead.
Someone superior calmly observes all this.
A few of us, golden boys, grinning at the rifles—
Does anybody know if we're actually mortal?

The wind would adorn our hair with dry leaves.
The sun, on the other hand, tries to make us mad.

We understand nothing and do everything wrong—
The very thing they'll bless us for later on.

2
They tried to buy us with love, but we couldn't sell
    ourselves,
Though our hands were obviously outstretched.
We went to glorious wars for shiny medals,
But when they were handed out, we fell asleep.

Yes, let someone say to whom it is we belong,
(since we are not our own.)

The one who knows is quiet as if still deliberating,
Though the decision surely has already been made.

DAY BEFORE IT BREAKS

The row of trees no longer leads to the well,
nor to the old castle.
It stops along the way,
and then absent-mindedly migrates into clouds.

Mistress, where is your door?
Where is the city in which we loved
and hated each other equally?
Once again our fate consists of
simple questions.

Outside the sentries thud. Neigh.
They lead the panic-stricken one
into towers of silence,
graze the vine of our jitters.
With some god on first name basis,
they overtake the day before it breaks.

Despair, then, separates
the few remaining bones.

SHOOTING AT DAWN

The rifles are loaded, the officer has only to finish
    the cigarette.
His green forehead glows in the dark with contempt.
What a rotten job this getting up before dawn!
If only there was money in it, (we know who profits here.)

The condemned man shook like a dry leaf,
A man without a name after whom no one will make a fuss.
He considers all these delays indecent.
Let it be done and over with as soon as possible.

They say, in the bush a nightingale felt like singing.
Singers are blind. It never suspected what was
    happening closeby.
In love with life, it gave itself to it greedily
With a song, fatal, heart-breaking and final.

FINAL NIGHT

I knew, when they depart, the jailer will return.
My love leaves the apartment, tiptoes down the stairs.
Then the jailer showed me the paper, but the darkness
    didn't know how to read
The executioner said to his wife: "I'd like some cooked pears,
    the kind we had when you were pregnant."
I guide you through the streets, love, you can't get lost.

My death first occurred within me; others can only repeat it.
"Tomorrow you'll die. I'll let you in on a secret: I write
    poetry."
The executioner grinned and the whole room turned bloody.
The jailer has his poems memorized and began saying them.
There are still three dark streets left before you get to
    my prison.

"I bit into her throat, but the teeth I felt in my own throat."
"They say," said the executioner to his wife, "that there are
    executioners even on the stars."
"I felt that my knee was her knee . . . " In the dark the jailer
    glowed purple like an apparition.
The rats peeked out. All these are his loves, I thought.
And when you stopped under the terrifying window, it started
    raining a little.

"The greatest danger for poetry is when it begins to mean
    something."
The rats were of different opinion but they couldn't express
    themselves.
"Symbols are like dampness," I said, "they must penetrate."
"God made the gallows and you're God's employee," said the
    executioner's wife.
I feel your sweet eyes all over my body like a warm bath.

The many that we'll remember in the moment of death; it seems,
    death exists just for that reason.
Actually, death is a respite before new mysterious adventures.
The rope of my still-unerected gallows couldn't sleep all
    night.

I can understand that. It's its first time.
The jailer said: "I'm thinking whether to let you smoke."

The executioner snored in his sleep and holy doves
    flew out of his mouth.
The jailer changed his mind: "I could pay dearly
    for those cigarettes."
To spite him, the rats brought out the butts from
    their holes.
"Go home sweetheart, you've got homework to do for
    tomorrow."
"You know, just last year I gave up smoking."

"I could've been spared this," said the jailer angrily.
And at daybreak, the gallows stood like young poplars.
"I hope you won't betray that I write poetry," said
    the worried jailer in parting.
The executioner strutted out dressed in the costume of
    an angel from the orphanage supply room.
I hope you were not late for school, love.

I CANNOT SAY THE NAME OF THE CITY

I cannot say the name of the city
Perhaps tomorrow I'll be killed at the hands of a friend
Perhaps drunk I'll betray his secret ways
Perhaps on all sides the spies lie in wait for me
Perhaps I will plant the firebomb in the main street
Perhaps the foundations beneath us are cracking

Perhaps heroes lose their courage in a decisive moment
Perhaps we have all forgotten why we started

The drunken wheel of fate turns
Blacksmiths forge shackles all night
Whores chase children away in the dark
The restless dead peer out of graves
And soon even the mad dogs will leave

Perhaps in their hurry they'll condemn me innocently
Perhaps I really did do something
Perhaps tonight I along with others will hang someone
Without a word someone who just happens along

I don't dare I can't I am not allowed
To say the name of the city

ALONE, FOR SUCH IS THE VICTORY

No longer afraid; I feel my wolf-teeth showing.
No longer the beaten path, for heaven's sake, bushes tempt me
    in the open field.
If my eyes flash, the crows flap their wings with contempt.

Not even houses, sidewalks or turnpikes,
Insatiable breasts reaching up after the snow.

I won't get lost, the winds point the goal.
Mine is on the other side.

No longer the question of time.
My doubled steps advance more quickly.
How prettily the lantern of my wolf-eye grins.

Hunters, already tonight I'll arrive
To the meadow that ate the tracks of the betrayer,
Calling to my mighty self in heaven,
Alone, for such is the victory.

MORNING

I wake in the morning blinded.
I hear only seams tearing.
Morning: cruel prince surrounded by hounds—
And beyond the window, the abyss.

Fingers (squads of ants) at some senseless labor
Which already belongs to the next world.
Footsteps—they're like gunfire
Into one's own flesh.

The whole earth looks like a slaughterhouse.
Here's somebody's skin, there a bloody thigh,
Horns, feet, guts, great innocent eyes,
Wide open to make it all appear more truthful.

Glasses of warm milk, glasses of blood,
Yours and mine mixed in the same meal of horror.
Streets strewn with broken glass.
Walls that attack with sharpened nails.

The bird that bursts like a grenade.

Morning like a slaughterhouse.
Its day like a clean butcher shop
To which dogs are prohibited entrance.

There's the hope of night, hope of the freezer.
Unless we are all sold out by then.

LARGE GRIEVING WOMEN

We are encircled by large grieving women.
In nights of solitude they grow even bigger,
at times, dividing secretly into two-three,
at times, joining again toward daybreak,

now already much too large, intended for some other world
    where passions are more generous.
Silently they gaze with their opaque eyes,
unable to fight back,
still one hears within them a pain, somewhat like the sound of
    stones rolling.

When they reach the unknown limit, they turn into mountains,
lie down at their own feet and become plains.
Whoever today walks over the earth forever gently brushes
    against women.

They flood over the heavens, too, a bit.
They are also the woods that stand on the horizon.
Everywhere their sedantary, already weary hugeness.

MASTER, BLOW OUT THE CANDLE

Master, blow out the candle, somber days are coming.
Better count the stars at night, sigh for lost youth.
Your disobedient words might bite through the leash.

Plant onions in your garden, chop wood, clean out the attic.
It's better that no one sees your eyes full of wonder.
That's how your craft is: there's nothing you can pass over
in silence.

If you can't stand it and some night again pick up the pen.
Master, be sensible, don't bother with prophesy.
Try to write the names of the stars instead.

The times are serious, nothing if forgiven to anyone.
Only clowns know the way you might pull through:
They cry when they feel like laughing and laugh when cries
rip their faces.

FLIGHT

Always the same road rain flash of lightning
Barefoot boy warrior singer all at once
Lover searching for his bed through the mist
The posse of waves drunken orgy of the crows above
I kept running over the sand while I did other things
Let the cities go to ruin behind my back
With the wind in pack in the direction of the wolves' flight
By the dunes the inspection of corpses
By the shucked corn again some hungry army
Wedding of smoke hearth and cannons
Ceaselessly resound in my bones
As I fall down and keep on running
Drunken fisherman holding a tatter of his net
At each step the dogs will get him
One bloody stone per each step
And a young woman with her breasts bared
Will the branch get her or the hunter the wanderer
Next to the lake that has its source in Hell
Sly lake with a noose of pearls
Lake of shallow hopes and bottomless betrayals
I who haven't turned around yet
Who am fear embodied I this small universe
Overripe the fruit that wrestles with worms
Next to the dread of fishes and chained hands of clams
A mother with her child and a destroyed cabin
Injustice you're constant like breathing
I jumped over glassy sands as over embers
Tomorrow and yesterday harmoniously mixed
Who would separate the years so happily coupled
Out of their bellies the centuries wail to each other
The sky has strewn itself over the clouds
Show me the difference belfries and gallows
Hear the drum-roll the human bones tolling alarm
It doesn't even reach to the top of the poplars
While in the sky the stars graze peacefully
Before they lower themselves into the milky sea-waves
And kiss the sinners where it's sweetest to kiss
But I kept running what I couldn't do is remember
Running I ate and I raped from time to time

I was even born running
With a scream following after the dazed millions
Falling dead I broke in half and ran in a pair
All of history falters in my knees
The unborn those hung and those that were given rifles
The separated lovers hungry chained
Blowing on empty fingers swollen drums
Next to lakes trenches graves
Every day heavier and darker in hope
Furrowed gouged like this fresco
Over the white scaffold of the treacherous sand

DRINKING SPREE
BENEATH THE OPEN SKY

How drunk I got tonight
That was some binge beneath the open sky
On the banks of the river where the fearful dare not go

The darkness swarmed with magicians
Like comets they hurled their fluttering cloaks through me
for a long while so that I was already choking

The river teemed with upturned fish and drowned fishermen

Absolutely no one bothered with me
While the meteors were falling into that posterior world
I must have been very small I must have been well-behaved

With my bottle of brandy and my short pants
With my skinny arms and my trimmed hair
With my large eyes that needed nothing

ELEGY

From the old settlements only the writings
remain. A large piece of yellow paper
stretches from south to north. It too
is beginning to rot. At midnight, the dirge
which only the stone-hearted one understands,
rustles into the dream. Senseless horror.
Meat falling off the bones
Weeping that will never reach its own cheek.

Wretched paper, parsimonous its explanation
of the end. Why even save anything
when from all the luxury only a clumsy drawing
remains? No one to take it in hand.
Even the bodies are no longer real.
They float on the edge of appearances.
A whole world deprived of its rights
dims within them. Next to it,
the one that conquered lasts a bit longer.
His purpose: to deny the existence of that
which in any case is no more.

IN THE NIGHT STEPS WAKE ME

In the night steps which haven't passed by
    wake me.
I find my hand by the window in reverie.
Color of the sky as if something supreme was
    happening.
The trees look much more solid and daring.

It could be love if love existed.
To the world that dream always remains,
Some sort of wild vegetation which mocks laws.
Wonderful to be her leaf.

My song, you be the flower of that freedom,
Unrestrained, with many visible and invisible
    petals,
Like gentle fingers for all the muffled sighs

Which at night call me to rescue them,
So that I take my pen and with its point open
    wounds—
Truly what you're seeing is my blood.

THE BEAUTY STEPS DOWN
FROM THE POSTER

It's autumn,
and the beauty steps down from the poster
waving her naked teats in greeting.

Everywhere fog and soot.
Quickly the beauty turns gray and yellow,
and trods with a soldier's step.

Naked army advances through ruins of reason.
Her nipples, belly, pubic triangle
become law and damnation.
The natives drop down like poisoned birds.

What could the poet's sensitivity do here.
He too lies raped on the metaphysical mud,
peeing in horror.

SCREAMS IN THE DARK

A scream that climbs a candle.
Great hollow scream above the feverish city.
The heavens now can be ripped open too.
Every moment we expect to hear the news:

nothing exists—except our troubles.
The stain of the scream on the shimmering table of midnight.
Useless the effort to move my fat fingers;
I'm choking—there's a scream around my neck.

The scream of the flower on the balcony
has already torn out its roots.
Soon even flowers won't know how to grow.
They'll run with us around the room.

The drunken scream of a man who in the dark
center of the world, (inside-out), discards parts
of whose existance he didn't know till now.
On the bottom he finds another homuncular self.

The scream of the window that no longer sees.
The scream of the clock that runs on screams.
Only yesterday we believed in the firm existence of
some other solution: that it doesn't matter

what we do, that someone else
will redeem our madness and then we'll
twist his neck. However, we found ourselves
utterly alone with our nakedness.

With the small hope in love.
With the even smaller hope in justice.
The scream of a lit cigarette in the night.
The scream of screams and the pale flame of a cry.

NOCTURN V

In darkness the centuries speak clearer.
The stone is in blossom.
The eyes find lost trees, shores.
The innards of the earth tremble.

The slain are slain more cleverly.
In darkness the wine renews its cheer.
Once again the dreamer is directed
to the garden of dreams.

How full the darkness is of sweet excess.
Birds fly out of the museum dust;
their bloody tracks can be seen by moonlight.
Real human sweat drops from the roof.

In darkness the prison door shuts more tightly.
Still, the fingers long to break them even more fiercely.
Every whisper echos like a struck anvil.
The heart is a clock on a high tower.

Petrified gods, perhaps, wake
and give anxiety back its meaning.

ATLANTIS

In heavy drink and in love,
especially under the effect of some old illness,
truly we see them hung from the sky:
three ships like three fairy godmothers.

We hear them distinctly, when the wind's howl
and the wildness of buxom waves—
at night, with the windows dimmed,
and the lewd whispers, in the hour of prayer,

when they're identical with our curses—
we hear them, discern them, but they never arrive
although they're always out there
just over the line of the horizon.

It's not for the sake of more space that they're coming to
        discover us.
Still, somehow they never reach our seas:
The armoured bow, the stern, the fluttering sails—
as if we were invisible, as if we didn't exist.

Fate seemingly unable to make up its mind.
Here History stops before our famous unreality;
alone we cannot break out of the magic circle,
held back as we are by our excessive gift of prophecy.

Never, never will we be discovered!
Never, never will we begin to exist!
Not even Columbus, not even a single Columbus will escape
        the curse.
The world will perish powerless before Atlantis.

THE MORNING ROAR OF THE CITY

Every morning you return from a long
voyage. Return out of some kind of death
and metamorphosis, where silently
the branches of your childhood sway,
and those others, even more hushed, that wait
beyond all existence. You leave behind
wisdom, the pure music of your body,
perhaps love, perhaps oblivion, perhaps
the bliss of tears. You leave your true self
which remains empty without worrying
that you won't be back again, since
it's the only one who knows for sure
whether you're there or here, where you sit
by the window and watch how in the sun's fire
the day itself returns with all its platoons.

The morning roar of the city grows,
at first terrifying, as if the murderer is
coming with his dogs and helpers—
then more and more bearable to your ears—
until you yourself, or someone else
awaken within you, and identical
doesn't begin himself to roar.

UNDER THE MICROSCOPE

You live under the microscope.
You go into a tavern, break glasses,
ashtrays, and the one above
darkly hunched over the lense,
grits his teeth. You phone a friend,
but there's somebody else on the line;
his heavy breathing gives him away.
He's sick of your long walks in the rain
nights by the open window, barefoot races
with the daybreak over the dew.

You play the comb and tissue paper and feel
he doesn't like it, doesn't know
how to interpret it. Perhaps
the song has a wicked intention?
Where's the key to the secret
whose doors were walled in? He's restless
on his chair, sweat drips off
his forehead onto the glass, his nerves
are strained, he's really gotten thin
the last few years and won't see a doctor.
Tightly he grips the microscope in hope

you'll fall first. And you blossom!
Transformed by the knowledge that you're dragging
someone else down to hell, someone so wise
that he knows you better than you know yourself
as a member of that species meant for gratuitous
extinction. You carouse. You go around
with whores. Gather nasty diseases.
And still you glow. How to tell him that in all that there's much
sense. It can be seen reflected

in his feverish eye, in the trembling
of his hand and that cough. The mouthing
                    of your words.

34

ON THE CARPET, STARING AT MYSELF

Some celebration.
One by one they all left me.
The last ones found it the hardest.
They suffered so much on account of themselves.

Then, my lightbulb left me,
And an assortment of other things.
Finally, even memory.

A beaten world rose up foolish with freedom,
And I, inordinately exalted to be its ruler,
Curl-up on the carpet and stare at myself.

Slavko Mihalić is regarded as one of the best poets now writing in Yugoslavia. Born in 1928, he has worked for many years as a journalist, an editor and publisher. He is the author of fourteen collections of poetry which have been translated in a number of European languages and for which he has received numerous prizes. The poems in this book cover his career from 1954 to the present. Mihalić lives in Zagreb.

Charles Simic is the author of many translations of Yugoslav poetry and a poet who has published nine books of poetry, the most recent of which are *Charon's Cosmology*, *Classic Ballroom Dances* and *Austerities*. For his translations of Vasko Popa he has received the P.E.N. Translation Prize, both from the American and the Yugoslav P.E.N. Club.

Peter Kastmiler is a young California poet who was born in East Germany of Yugoslav parents. He's the author of two volumes of his own poetry: *When the Creature is Silent* 1973 and *Moon Behind Mountain*. He has translated many of the leading contemporary Yugoslav poets, and has an anthology of Croatian poetry ready. He lives in Oakland.